AMAZING MINECRAFT ACTIVITY BOOK

GAMEPLAY PUBLISHING

SPOT THE DIFFERENCE

Steve took two screenshots of a day in the village! Unfortunately, an Enderman drew all over it. Find 5 differences between the pictures.

THE PICKAXE SHOP

Steve is at the village shop looking for a new pickaxe! The only problem is there are 5 different types to choose from. Can you help him find what each type of pickaxe is good for?

1. Diamond Pickaxe e _____.
2. Gold Pickaxe   _____.
3. Iron Pickaxe   _____.
4. Stone Pickaxe   _____.
5. Wood Pickaxe   _____.

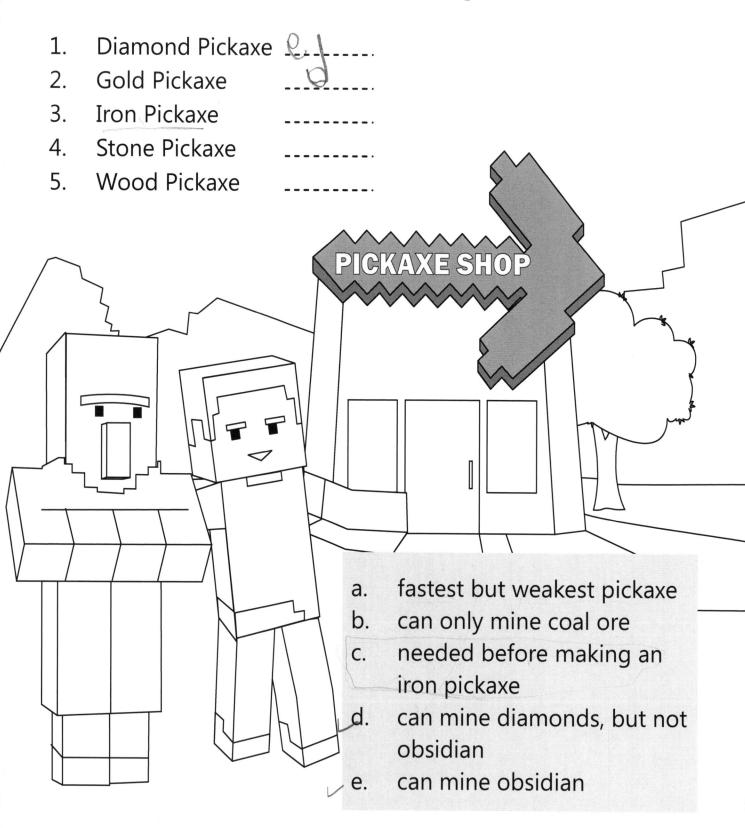

a. fastest but weakest pickaxe
b. can only mine coal ore
c. needed before making an iron pickaxe
d. can mine diamonds, but not obsidian
e. can mine obsidian

WHO?

Join up the dots in number order to see who is lurking in the cave.

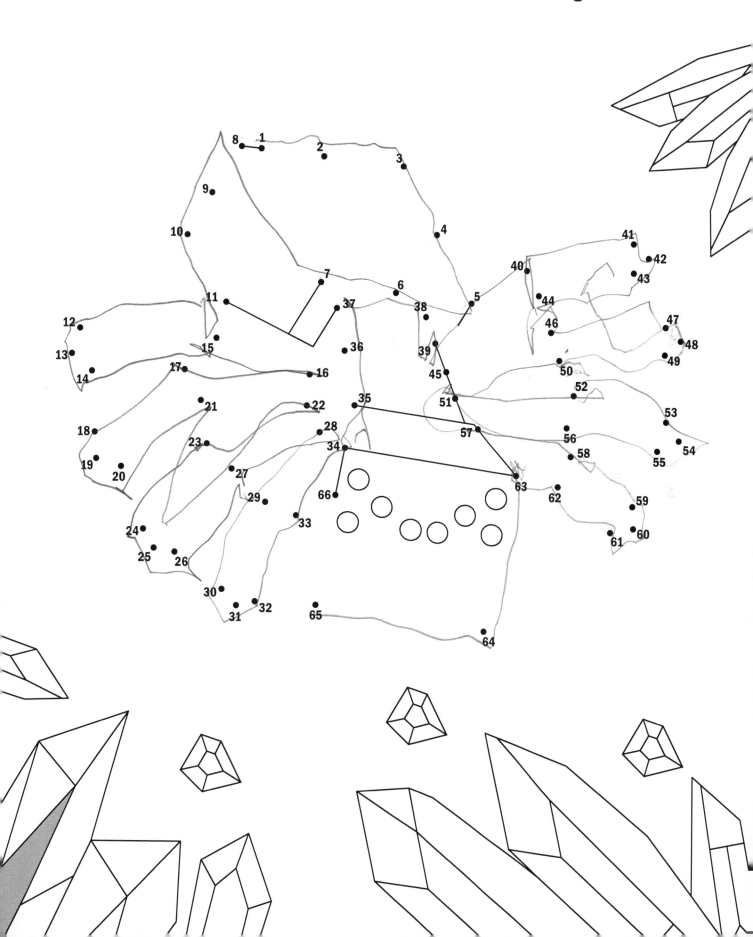

NETHER PARKOUR

CaptainSparklez is running away from ghasts and needs to get to his portal quickly. The path to the portal is over a sea of lava. Help him find the way back to the portal.

HIDDEN PICTURE

Shade in the shapes that have a square to show a very powerful mob.

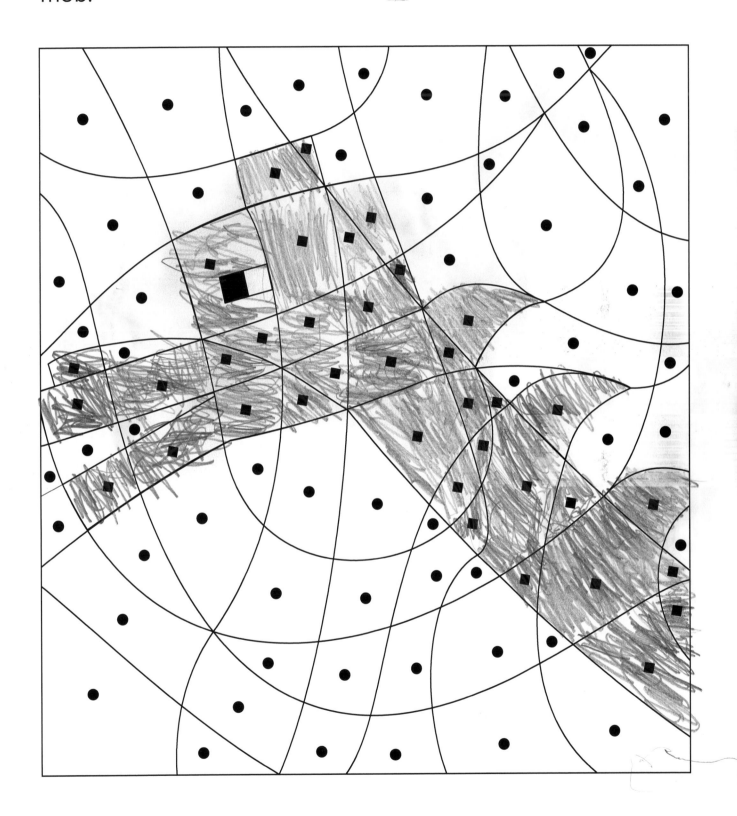

OCEAN MONUMENT MAZE

While exploring the new Ocean Monument, Matt got lost in the underwater passageways! Can you help him find his way back to the entrance before his water-breathing potion runs out?

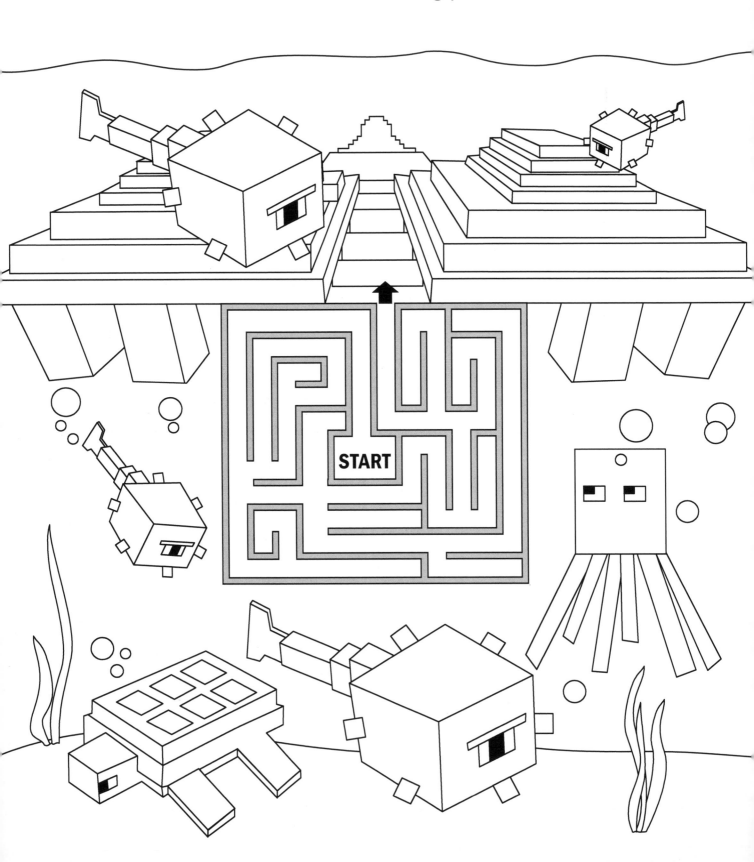

ENDERMAN PRANK

Steve took a nap on his island base. While he was asleep an Enderman came and moved some things! Circle 5 differences in the bottom picture to help Steve figure out what has been moved?

RARE BIOMES

Steve took notes about rare biomes he encountered on his adventures, but his notes got mixed up when he fell into a cave. Can you help him match the biomes with the correct descriptions?

1. Mesa   ---------
2. Extreme Hills   ---------
3. Mushroom Island ---------
4. Swamp   ---------
5. Savannah   ---------
6. Mega Taiga   ---------

Answers:

a. the only biome where podzol block naturally generates
b. a type of biome where horses and villages can be found
c. this biome is always near an ocean and does not spawn any hostile mobs
d. stained clay and red sand can be found in this biome
e. this biome contains many slimes and lilypads
f. this biome has emerald ore and silverfish

MINECRAFT BAKE OFF

Find and circle all worlds related to baking in Minecraft.

```
J H X R R C J T R D P G O Q K
M W Y N D O E A A C C O O L T
C W N W N H G E C O O K I E V
D F F P O U R C E P P M O B X
X E H Z S B S C A K E I F C N
P U M P K I N B R V O A L E N
D I H B C B U E G D D Y W X G
P J D C N B L K G V S C H G S
J F R O U W C O B O N M E C J
T I P U M P K I N P I E A X O
K P W O W L W S V U C W T Q F
L N Y C P J C D I S I H F F Q
S X F Y M D H M A L W G G Q J
H F S A M P X R Z K A P K P U
C P N S B G L J I S X T K A T
```

BREAD
CAKE
COOKIE
EGG
MILK
PUMPKIN
PUMPKIN PIE
SUGAR
WHEAT

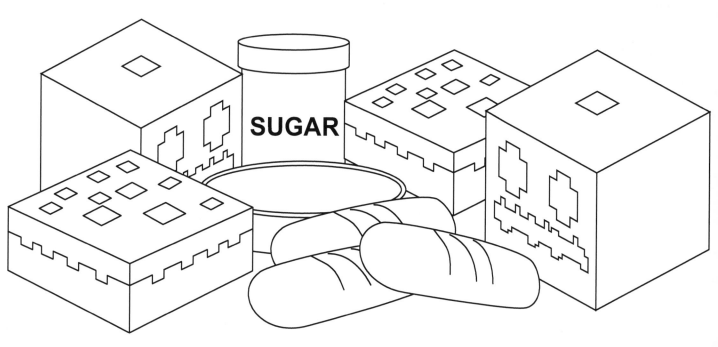

SUGAR

SPECIAL MOBS

Today Steve is learning about special mobs. Can you help him identify which characteristic belongs with each monster below?

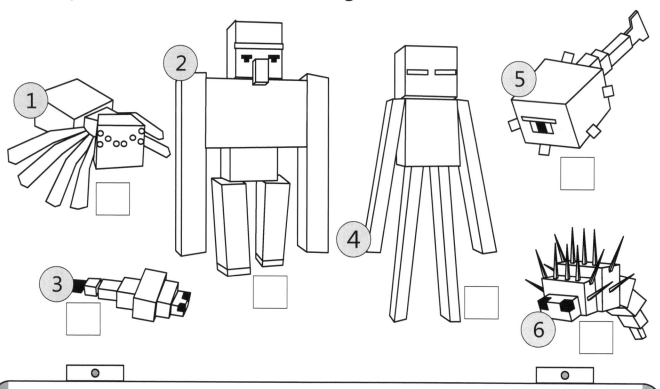

Characteristics:

a. A mob that can climb walls
b. A tall, dark monster with twice the health of Steve that can move blocks
c. A small arthropod that can burrow and hide itself in rocks
d. A small monster that sometimes spawns during teleportations
e. A powerful mob that protects villagers from zombie attacks
f. A swimming mob that can shoot a powerful laser

MAGIC PICKAXE

Steve is mining underground! Help him find ore by solving the puzzle.

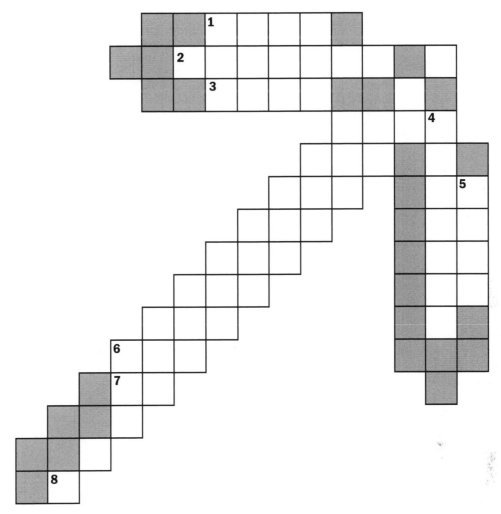

Across:
1. A useful fuel source
2. The strongest and most precious material
3. A rare ore used to create tools that are less durable than wood.

Down:
4. A villager's favorite ore for trading
5. The most common ore used to create tools and armor.

Diagonally:
6. Emits red glow and can be obtained by killing witches
7. An ore used as a dye
8. An ore that can be found in the Nether

SKELETON ATTACK

Steve is under skeleton attack! In order to fire back at them, he needs to craft a bow and arrows. A bow requires 3 sticks and 3 strings, while 4 arrows can be crafted from a flint, a feather and a stick.

1) How many arrows can Steve craft with 12 sticks, 12 feathers and 12 flints?

Answer: _ _ _ _ _ _ _ _ _ _ _ _ _ _ _ _ _

2) If 3 arrows are needed to take down one skeleton and assuming that Steve won't miss a shot, how many skeletons can Steve take down with 16 arrows?

Answer: _ _ _ _ _ _ _ _ _ _ _ _ _ _ _ _ _

3) Steve has 16 arrows, 4 sticks, 3 feathers and 12 flints. If he decides to craft additional arrows, how many arrows in total will he have?

Answer: _ _ _ _ _ _ _ _ _ _ _ _ _ _ _ _ _

NETHER SURVIVAL

Jim is lost in the Nether! Can you help him find his way back to the Nether Portal?

CHALET HIDEOUT

Stampy plans to build a wooden chalet and he wants to use base species of trees. Help him find various tree types to construct his chalet.

Across:

3. Only found in roofed forest biomes and can also drop apples
6. Gives a white colored log
7. A PE exclusive tree with logs covered in vines.

Down :

1. Commonly known as pine tree
2. The only tree that can grow into any other leaf block
4. Found in Savanna biome
5. Tallest tree type

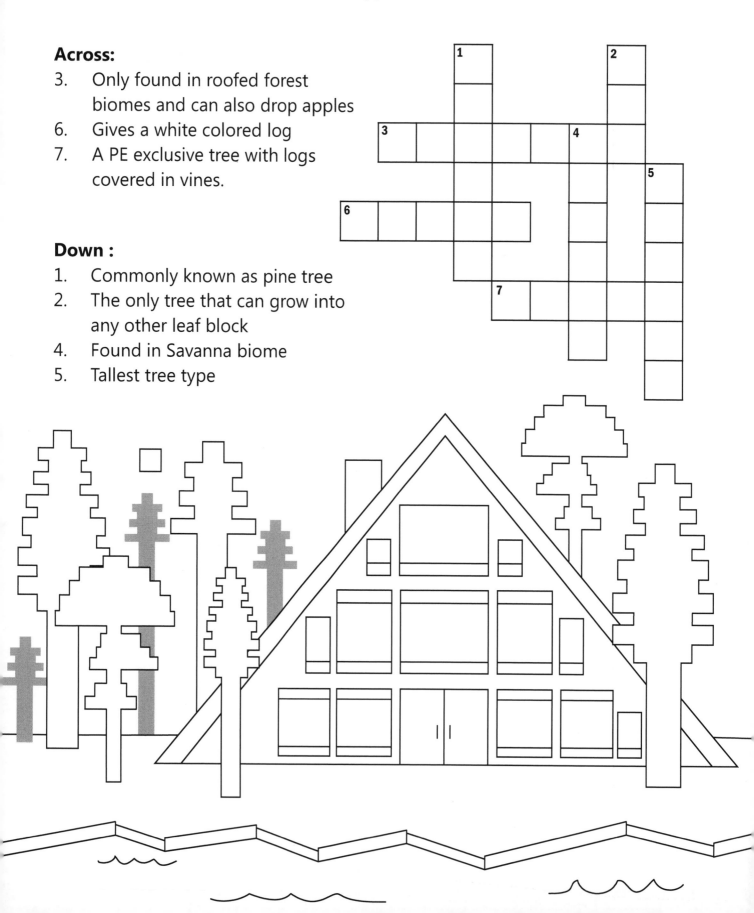

MARKET DAY

If you take 10 emeralds to trade with a farmer villager and buy everything on the shopping list at the bottom of the page, how many emeralds will you have left?

1 emerald for 2 loaves

BREAD LOAF

1 emerald for 6 cookies

COOKIES

1 emerald for 5 apples

APPLES

1 emerald for 2 pies

PUMPKIN PIE

1 emerald for 1 cake

CAKE

Shopping List

4 Loaves of bread

10 Apples

3 Cakes

6 Cookies

2 Pumpkin pies

Answer:

- - - - - - - - - - - - -

BLURRY VISION

Steve is exploring alone at night. His vision is blurry because he forgot to drink a night vision potion. Help him find 5 differences in the bottom picture.

17 NETHER WART MAZE

Jack lost his dog in the Nether Wart maze! Help him find his dog but make sure that he does not step into the icky soul sand.

ENDER DRAGON DIGITS

See if you can fill in the missing numbers on the Ender Dragon's spikes.

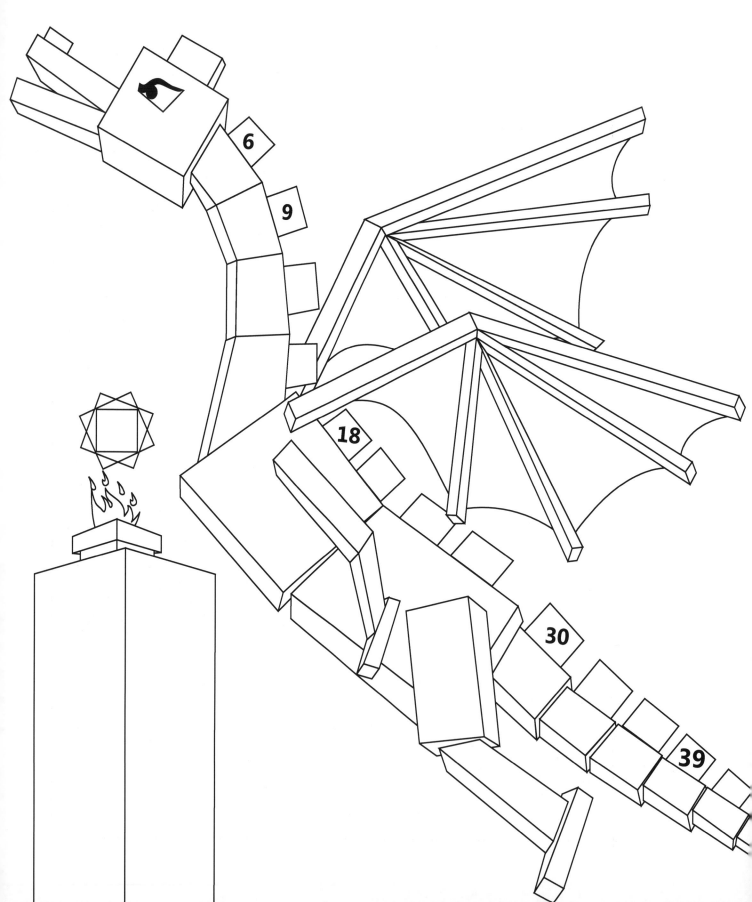

TRIANGLE ART

Shade in the triangles below to see a hostile mob which can climb ladders and is afraid of wolves.

MUDDLED BIOMES

See if you can unscramble these biome names.

1. aaiTg ....

2. oretsF ....

3. retesD ....

4. aseM ....

5. gnuJel ....

6. wpnadaSlm ....

7. aaanvSn ....

8. rnezFo naecO ....

9. xEemter ilslH ....

10. homrusMo dnalsI ....

SKELETON DUEL

Sky saved two identical screenshots of his duel with a skeleton but one file got corrupted. Help Sky find 7 differences between the two files.

HEDGE MAZE

Steve and his villager friend were exploring a hedge maze and have gotten separated. Help Steve reunite with his villager friend!

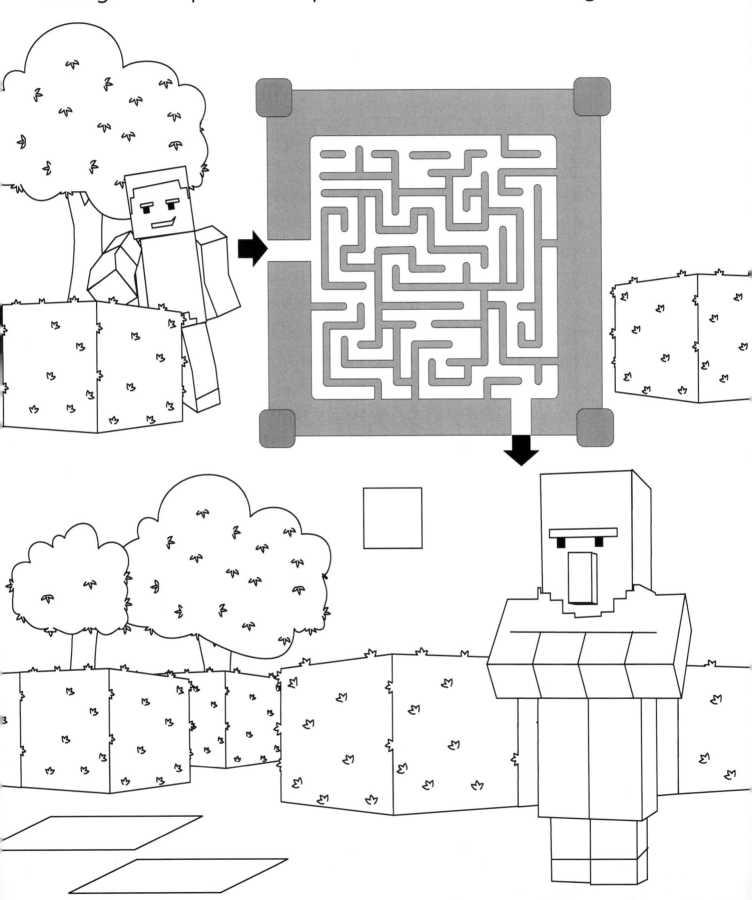

UNDER THE OCEAN

Join up the dots in number order to discover mobs that spawn in water.

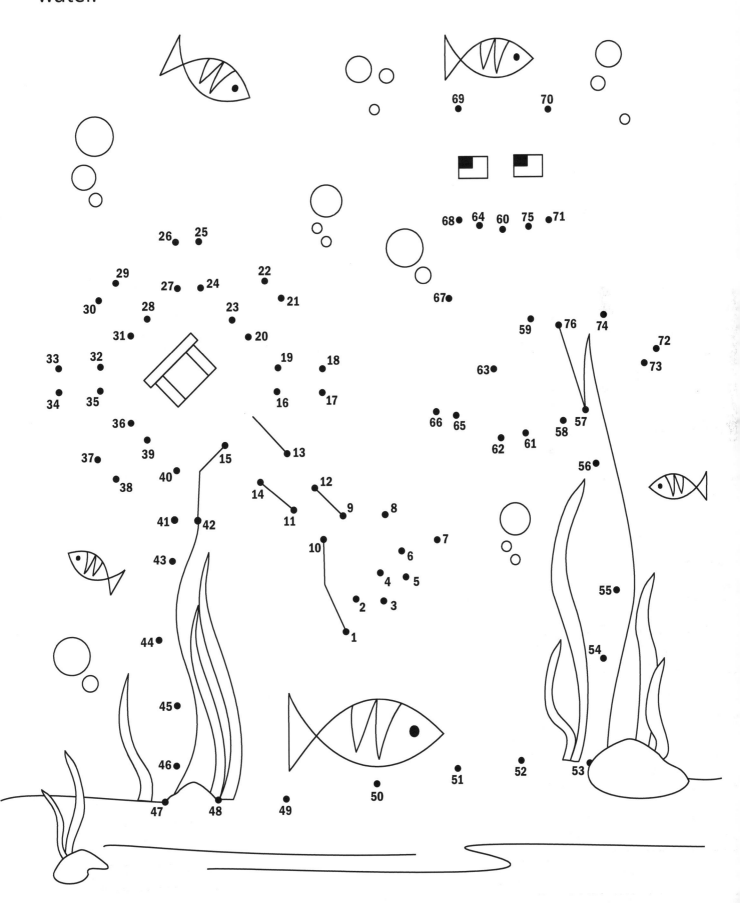

DOUBLE VISION

Copy the drawings across into the blank spaces to see two complete pictures of a hostile mob that uses splash potions as weapon.

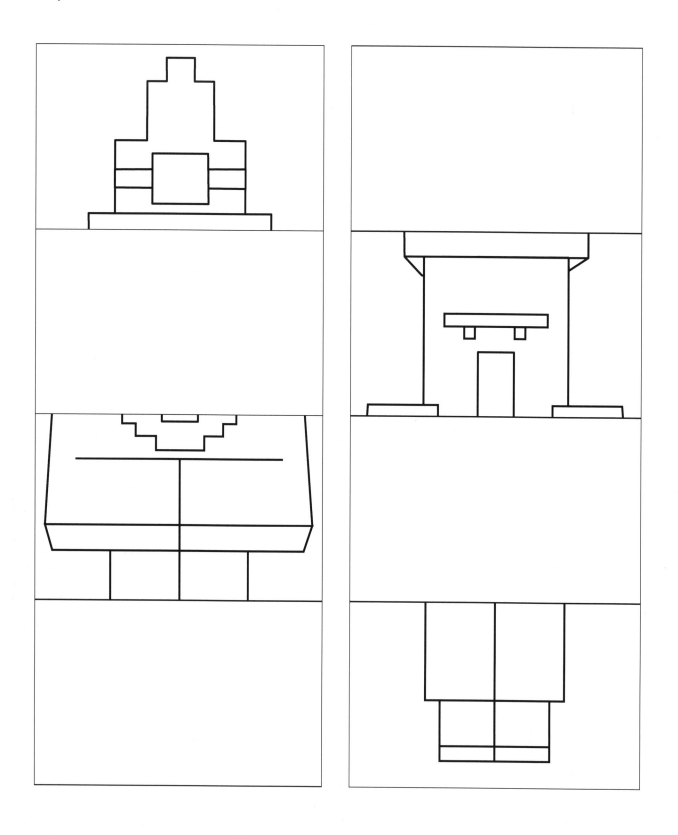

FARMING COMPETITION

Steve wants to become a farmer! Help him create the biggest farm by planting all variety of crops.

Across:

5. A food crop that you can use as a mask
7. A crop that can poison players for 4 seconds
8. Useful for making bread
9. Used to breed pigs
10. Grows on jungle wood blocks

Down :

1. A Minecraft PE exclusive crop
2. Drops slices when harvested
3. Can make paper out of it
4. Can be obtained by shearing a mooshroom
6. A crop that can be baked in furnace

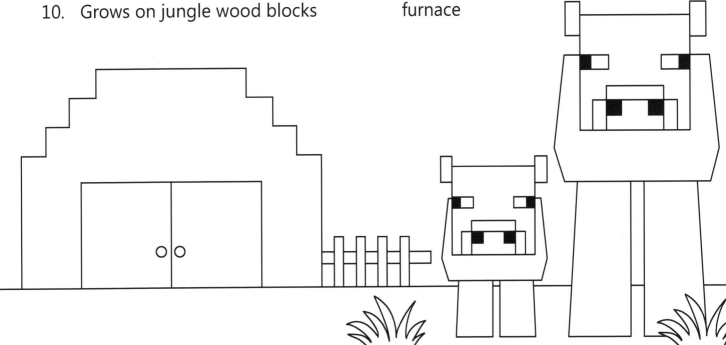

SPIDER ATTACK

Mike is lost underground! After walking for a few minutes, he finds another cave just like the one he came from! Can you help him find 7 differences between the two caves?

BREWING INGREDIENTS

Hannah wants to make some potions. She labeled and placed several ingredients on the table. Help her write down the name of the right ingredient that goes into each potion below.

1. Regeneration Potion _____
2. Healing Potion _____
3. Poison Potion _____
4. Fire Resistence Potion _____
5. Night Vision Potion _____
6. Strength Potion _____
7. Water Breathing Potion _____
8. Speed Potion _____
9. To corrupt a potion's effect _____

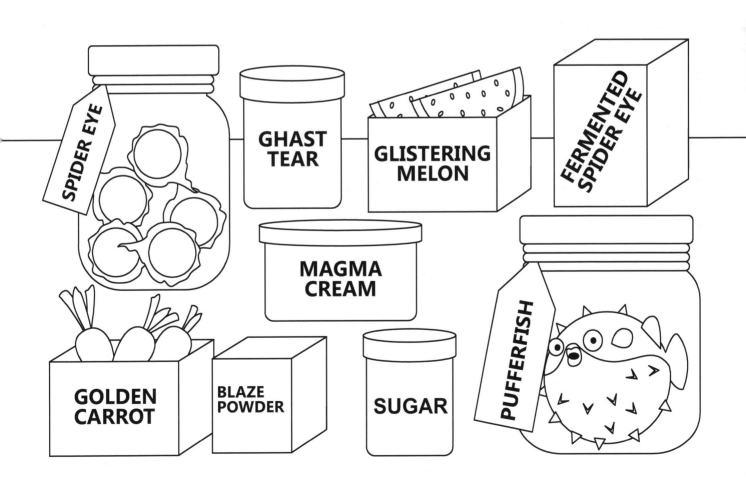

GIANT ENDERMAN

Draw a new Endermen on the grid, exactly the same shape but twice as big. The first path has been done for you.

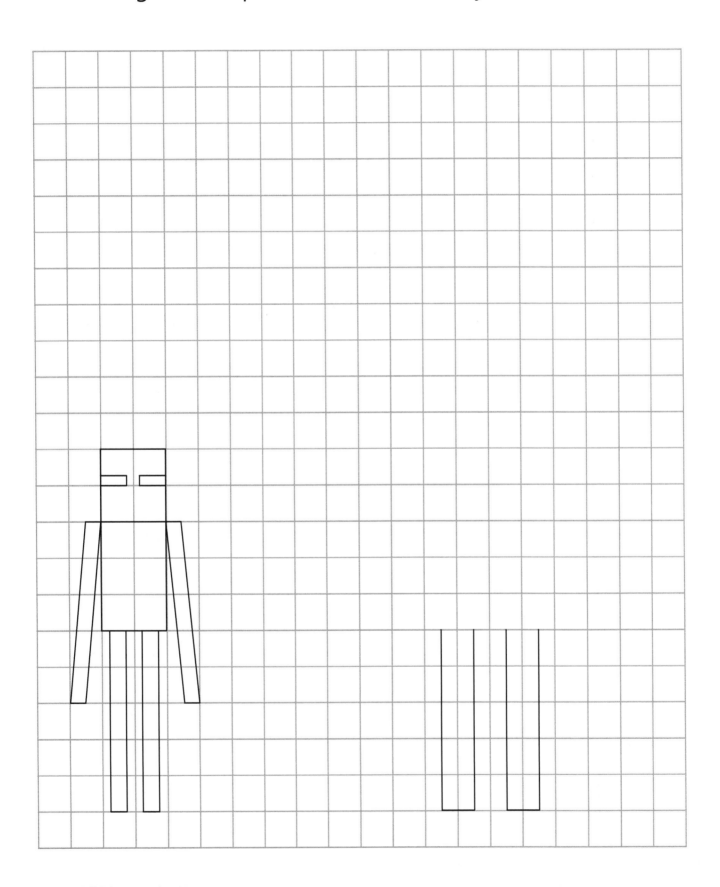

TRADING WITH VILLAGERS

Seth wants to sell some of his things to the villagers for emeralds! Can you figure out who will buy each type of item?

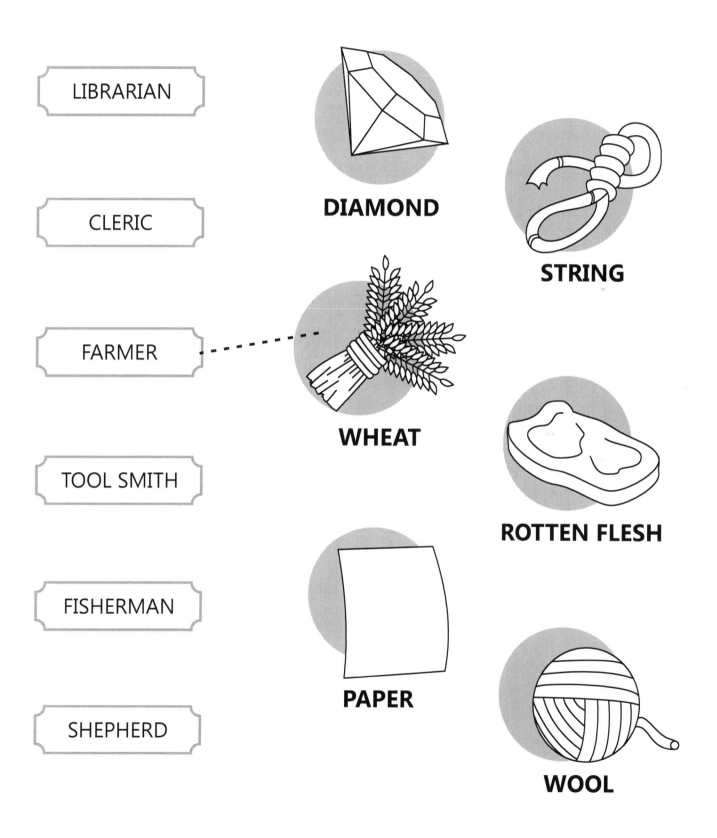

LIBRARIAN

CLERIC

FARMER

TOOL SMITH

FISHERMAN

SHEPHERD

DIAMOND

STRING

WHEAT

ROTTEN FLESH

PAPER

WOOL

VILLAGER BLACKSMITH

Cross out all the letters in the grid that appear more than once to reveal an item which can be found in the blacksmith's chest.

B	K	Q	A	E	M	L	K
Z	N	F	H	X	P	U	J
C	L	G	Y	B	D	I	X
I	P	J	G	R	V	N	A
X	X	U	O	Q	T	P	U
V	T	W	A	I	F	C	I
G	S	T	Y	K	B	M	J
Q	N	H	E	L	Z	V	B

WITHER FIGHT

A wither has been summoned in the Nether Fortress. Help Steve find the wither boss so he can fight it and get a Nether Star!

RAW FOOD

Steve is extremely hungry. Help him find some food in the wild that he can eat raw without any cooking or crafting.

Across:

4. Get it by breaking oak leaves
7. Dropped by zombies
8. Obtained from melon blocks
9. Dropped by cows when they die
10. Fish that cannot be cooked
11. Brewing ingredient obtained through fishing
12. Used to breed rabbits
13. Raw food dropped by sheep upon death

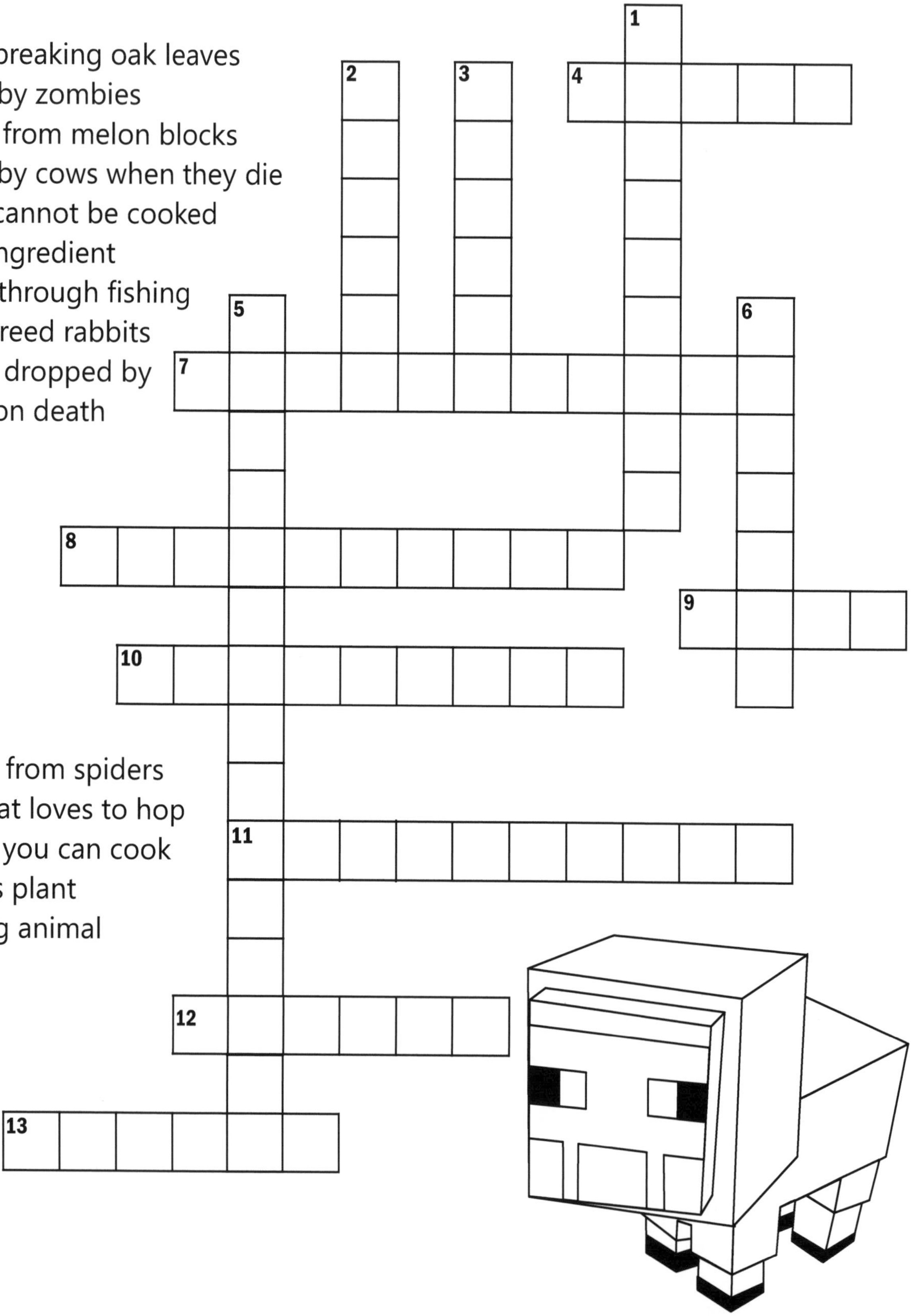

Down:

1. Can get it from spiders
2. Animal that loves to hop
3. A red fish you can cook
5. Poisonous plant
6. Egg-laying animal

STAMPY'S LOVELY WORLD

Find out which 6 letters of the alphabet are missing from this page, then unscramble them to find out what is Stampy's favorite place in Stampy's Lovely World.

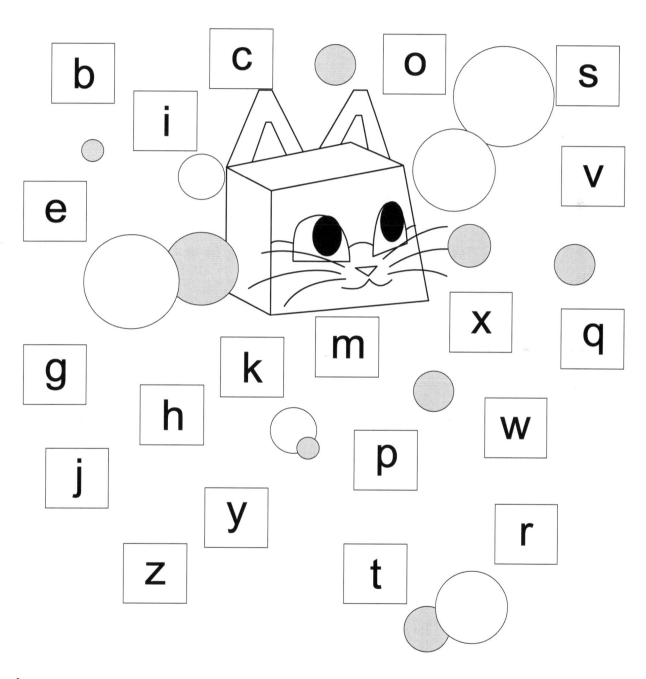

Answer: _ _ _ _ _ _ _ _ _ _ _ _

CONQUER THE STRONGHOLD

Lewis has finally found his first stronghold! Help him explore its deep passageways and find the End Portal. Try not to get caught in any cobwebs or be bitten by the silverfish!

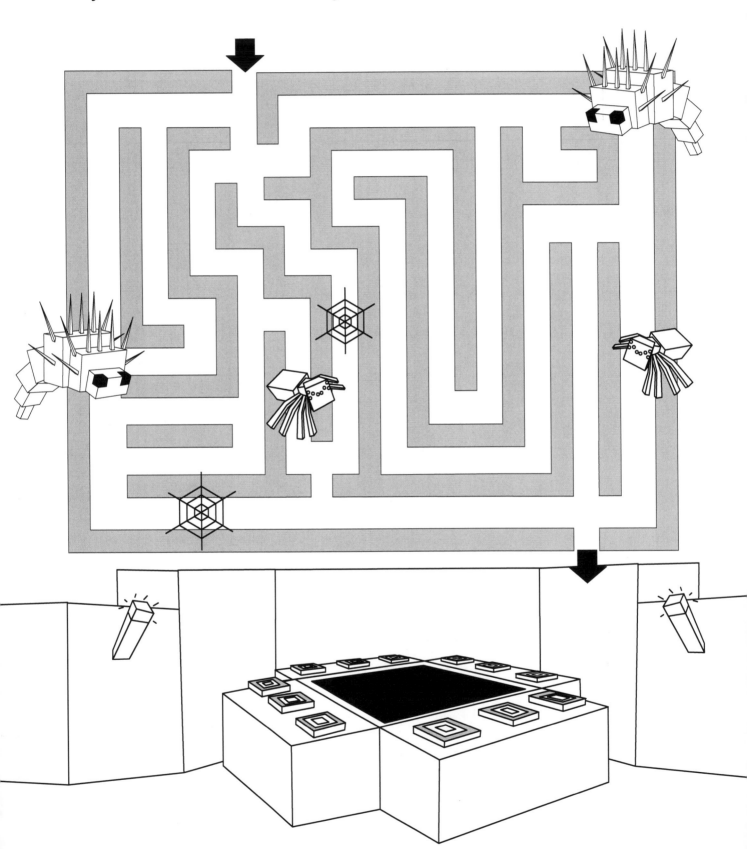

MINECRAFT ARMORY

Lewis and Simon from Yogscast built a massive armory. Find the names of the items you may find in their armory. The words could be written horizontally, vertically or even diagonally!

```
F N J B E S F I F I L E X M T
D O N O W C H E S T P L A T E
D F S W T L U T H H N Q S S A
W Q C I X A K E E X V C G F Y
U K J P Q V V Z P A I N R R V
P P B O K A E M C O I E L Q D
X G J B O O T S D G C S G R S
M F O Z N O H W G A D K A O W
Z E T X H K O E N N F J S X O
K U S F V R L R L A R M O R R
Z A S J R I U F H M J F T D D
I S Z A V F E F W Z E N U G D
E J Y N Z X A H S H C T N V T
S Q A V W J Z U V J L F I O P
J U D N U W W Q N R Y H C S Z
```

ARMOR
LEGGINGS
HELMET
CHESTPLATE
BOOTS
TUNIC
SWORD
BOW
ARROW
FURNACE
ANVIL
LAVA

DOUBLE VISION

Copy the drawings across into the blank spaces to see two complete pictures of a utility mob that defends villagers.

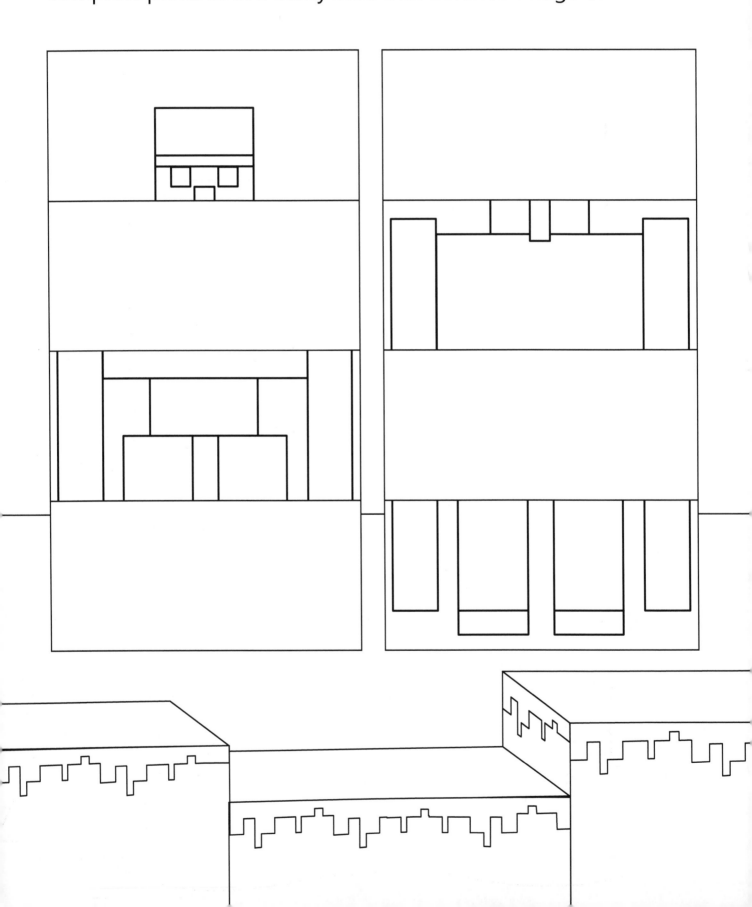

FOREST MAZE

Steve wants to go to the lake on the other side of the forest to get a bucket of water. Help him find his way through the forest.

POTION BREWING

James needs to know how to get ingredient for his potions. Can you help him figure out how each ingredient is obtained?

1. Magma cream ----
2. Blaze powder ----
3. Golden carrot ----
4. Glistering melon ----
5. Ghast tear ----
6. Spider eye ----
7. Sugar ----
8. Fermented spider eye ----
9. Pufferfish ----

a. a rare catch from fishing
b. dropped by a large flying Nether mob
c. a rare drop from an 8 legged monster
d. crafted from a crop found in villages and 8 golden nuggets
e. obtained from a plant that grows next to water
f. crafted from a plant found in the jungle
g. crafted from an item dropped by blazes
h. crafted from two of the ingredients on the list and a brown mushroom
i. crafted using drops of blazes and slimes

OCELOT FRIEND

Number the blocks at the bottom in alphabetical order, then copy their shapes into the grid to make a picture.

1	2	3
4	5	6

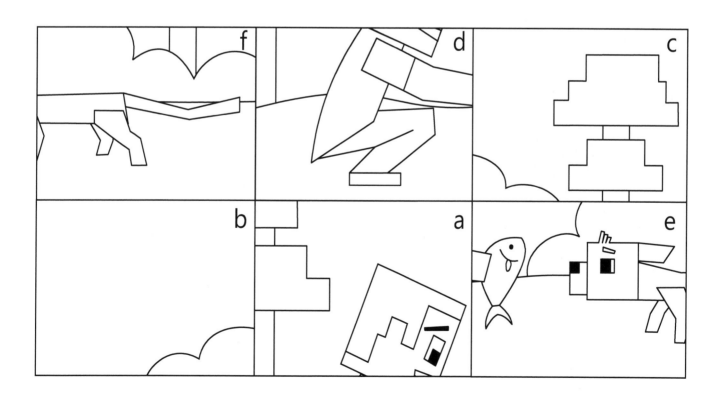

FURNACE FUEL

Steve is running low on fuel for his furnace. Help him find items to burn so he can have his steak!

Across:

3. Decorative block with books
5. Commonly used as enclosure for mobs
8. Acquired by defeating blazes
12. Used to go up or down a block without having to jump
13. A block used as a horizontal door
14. Can be created by putting wood in the crafting grid
15. A block used for storing other blocks and items
16. Known as half-block

Down :

1. A block that plays a note when activated
2. A block used to detect mobs
4. Used to play music discs
6. An item that can be grown into trees
7. Essential block that has crafting grid
9. Obtained by burning wood
10. Created from 2 wooden planks
11. Most effective fuel source
15. The only mineral that can be used as fuel

ABANDONED MINESHAFT

Peter is exploring an abandoned mineshaft! Help him find the treasure chest and his way out!

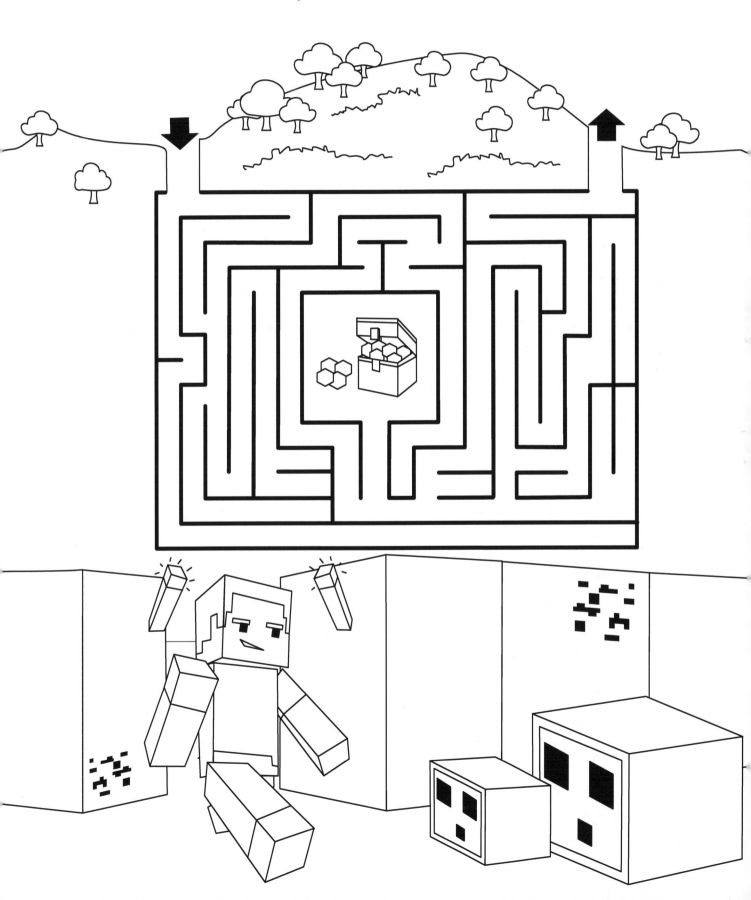

BAKING MARATHON

Steve is baking cakes for a party in the village! A cake requires 3 buckets of milk, 1 egg, 2 units of sugar and 3 units of wheat to make. Each cake has 6 slices.

1) How many cakes can Steve make with 7 buckets of milk, 2 eggs, 6 units of sugar and 8 units of wheat?

Answer: ------------------

2) If Steve wants to make 3 cakes and has only 4 buckets of milk, how many more buckets of milk will he have to get?

Answer: ------------------

3) If there are 13 villagers and 6 cakes, how many slices of cake can each villager get, if they all have an equal number of slices? How many slices will be left over?

Answer: ------------------

STAMPY'S BUILDINGS

Find the names of the places and buildings created in Stampy's Lovely World series. They may be written horizontally or vertically.

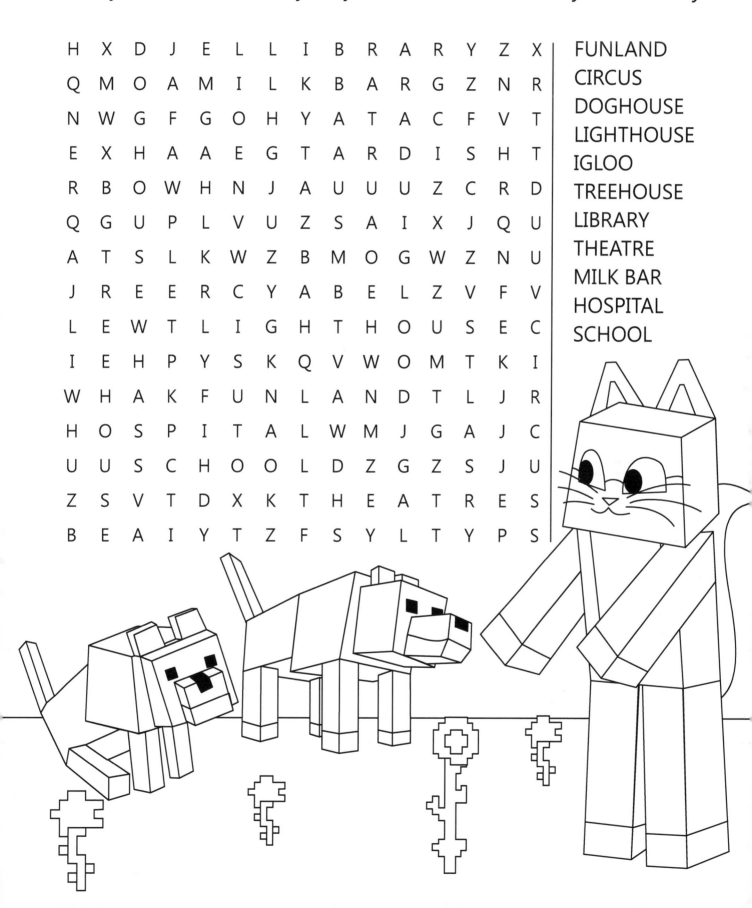

```
H X D J E L L I B R A R Y Z X
Q M O A M I L K B A R G Z N R
N W G F G O H Y A T A C F V T
E X H A A E G T A R D I S H T
R B O W H N J A U U U Z C R D
Q G U P L V U Z S A I X J Q U
A T S L K W Z B M O G W Z N U
J R E E R C Y A B E L Z V F V
L E W T L I G H T H O U S E C
I E H P Y S K Q V W O M T K I
W H A K F U N L A N D T L J R
H O S P I T A L W M J G A J C
U U S C H O O L D Z G Z S J U
Z S V T D X K T H E A T R E S
B E A I Y T Z F S Y L T Y P S
```

FUNLAND
CIRCUS
DOGHOUSE
LIGHTHOUSE
IGLOO
TREEHOUSE
LIBRARY
THEATRE
MILK BAR
HOSPITAL
SCHOOL

SHREDDED NOTE

Alex left a message for his friend, but it has been torn up by a griefer. Find the missing endings, then write them down to see what was in the note.

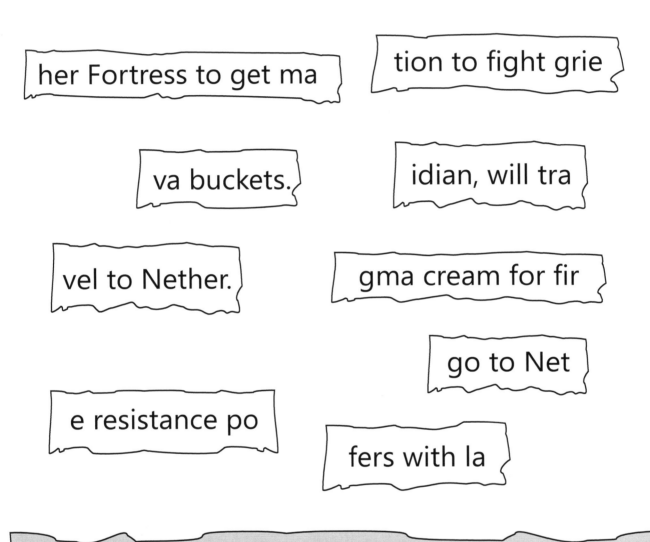

her Fortress to get ma

tion to fight grie

va buckets.

idian, will tra

vel to Nether.

gma cream for fir

go to Net

e resistance po

fers with la

Gone mining obs _____.

Need to _____

_____

_____.

TREASURE CHEST

Steve has been investigating an abandoned mineshaft. He found a chest with 57 units of different ores.

- He has 12 lumps of coal and 3 gold ingots
- He has 4 less diamonds than coal
- He has twice as much lapis lazuli as diamonds
- The number of iron ingots is equal to the number of coal lumps and gold ingots added together. The rest is red-stone.

How much of each item did he find?

| Coal .... | Gold .... |

| Diamonds .... | Lapis Lazuli .... |

| Iron .... | Redstone .... |

WHO?

46

Join up the dots in number order to discover a useful passive mob.

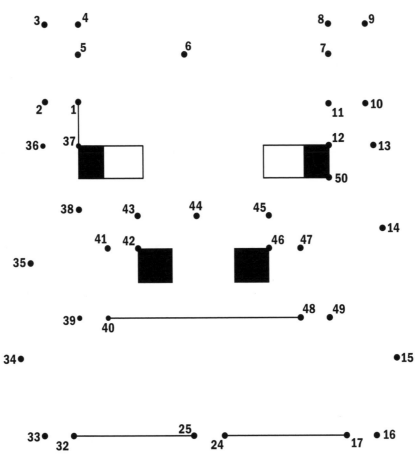

FLOWER GARDEN

Dave is creating a garden! Help him find different flowers that grow in the world of Minecraft.

Across:

3. A flower with many colour variations
5. A red flower which rhymes with puppy
6. Always faces east
8. Has red flowers and thorns
9. Can be used to breed rabbits
11. Only spawns in flower forest

Down :

1. A white flower used to craft light gray dye
2. Grows naturally in a swamp biome
4. Has white petals and yellow disc in the middle
7. Can be used to create pink dye
10. Can be used to craft magenta dye

1) Steve will be journeying to the Nether for 60 minutes. How many 8-minute Fire Resistance potions he should bring to be protected from lava the entire time?

Answer: _____

2) If he will only be traveling in the Nether for 40 minutes, how many 3-minute Fire Resistance potions he should bring to protect himself from lava the entire time?

Answer: _____

3) If Steve will fight the Wither for 15 minutes, how many 3-minute Regeneration potions and 8-minute Strength potions he needs to make to have Strength and Regeneration during the entire fight?

Answer: _____

NETHER FORTRESS LOOT

Andy is looking for the Nether Fortress loot. Help him find it and then safely get out of the fortress as wither skeletons and blazes are always ready to attack.

VILLAGER PROFESSIONS

Steve wants to trade with the villagers for some valuable items. Can you help him figure out which villager profession sells what?

1. Farmer   --------------------------------------
2. Leatherworker --------------------------------------
3. Armorer   --------------------------------------
4. Fletcher   --------------------------------------
5. Cleric   --------------------------------------
6. Librarian   --------------------------------------

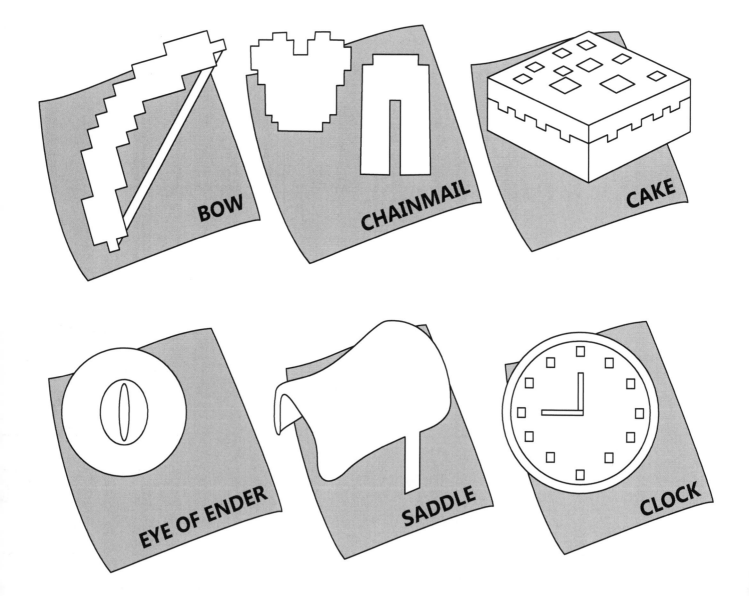

BOW

CHAINMAIL

CAKE

EYE OF ENDER

SADDLE

CLOCK

MINECRAFT YOUTUBERS

Find the names of famous Minecraft youtubers. They may be written horizontally or vertically.

```
S M S N H X S D I A E E F F C
V Q M L E W I S B N S V S A A
P M E M B N J T A W I Y S N P
E R S N A F G A L A P P L Z T
V D K A J V C M L W S O A E A
W O Y Y A V A P I E T E M A I
T B S O N Y N Y S M R Z A B N
R S B G C I P L T C K N C D S
Q S N S A B I O I R B M O F P
U U K C N U C N C N S J W L A
U N O A A A U G S X D V K D R
W D A S D W A H Q T K R Y Y K
K E G T I V O E U X S Q C F L
Z E Y G A Q S A I B H W K U E
Z G E X N L C D D X L F L O Z
```

STAMPYLONGHEAD
SKY
YOGSCAST
LEWIS
CAPTAINSPARKLEZ
SSUNDEE
SLAMACOW
BAJANCANADIAN
SIPS
IBALLISTICSQUID

CAVE CHALLENGE

Duncan is lost in a cave. A cave spider chased him down a dark tunnel and now he can't find his way back to the entrance of the cave. Help him find his way out, but be careful of the spiders' poisonous bites!

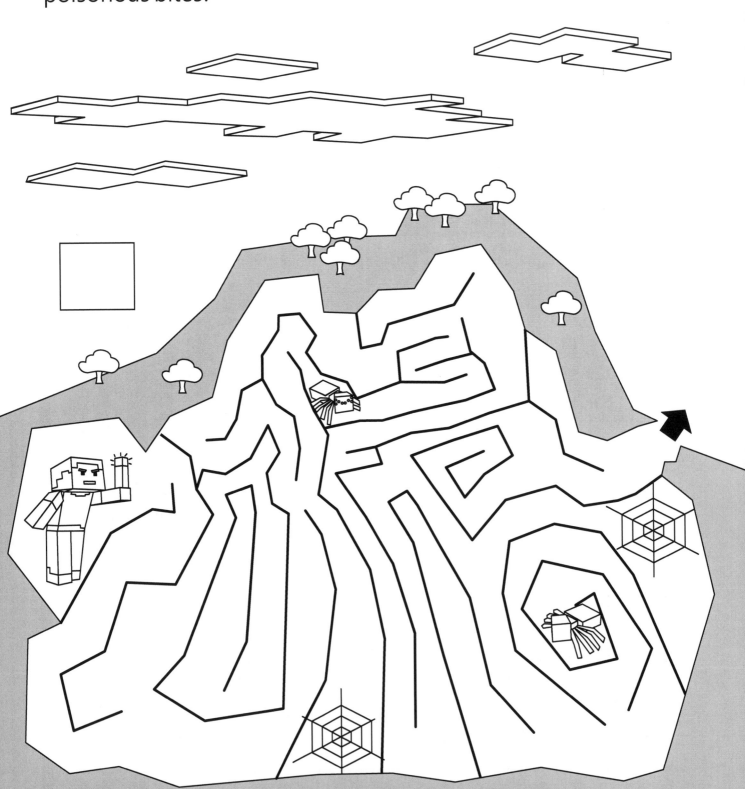

OVERWORLD HOSTILE MOBS

Andrew's home is under attack! Solve the crossword to help him identify the invaders.

Across:
1. A type of hostile rabbit
4. Uses splash potions as a weapon
7. Undead villager
8. A bouncing cube monster
9. Undead mob equipped with bows
10. Explodes when close to player

Down :
2. Spawns when an ender pearl is thrown
3. Spawns from monster eggs
5. A skeleton mob on top of a spider
6. A baby zombie on top of a chicken
7. Undead mob that groans

ARMOR STRENGTH

Diamond armor reduces damage by 80%. Iron armor reduces damage by 60%. Steve's sword does 5 hearts of damage per hit.

1) Steve wants to attack a diamond-armored enemy with 10 hearts of health, how many hits will it take to destroy the enemy?

Answer: ------------------

2) How many hits would it take Steve to destroy an iron-armored enemy with 10 hearts of health?

Answer: ------------------

3) How many times better is diamond armor than iron armor?

Answer: ------------------

DESERT TEMPLE MAZE

Harry found a desert temple buried in the sand. Help him navigate through the passageways to find a chest full of diamonds!

VILLAGE LIFE

Find the words in the list below. They may be written horizontally, vertically or even diagonally!

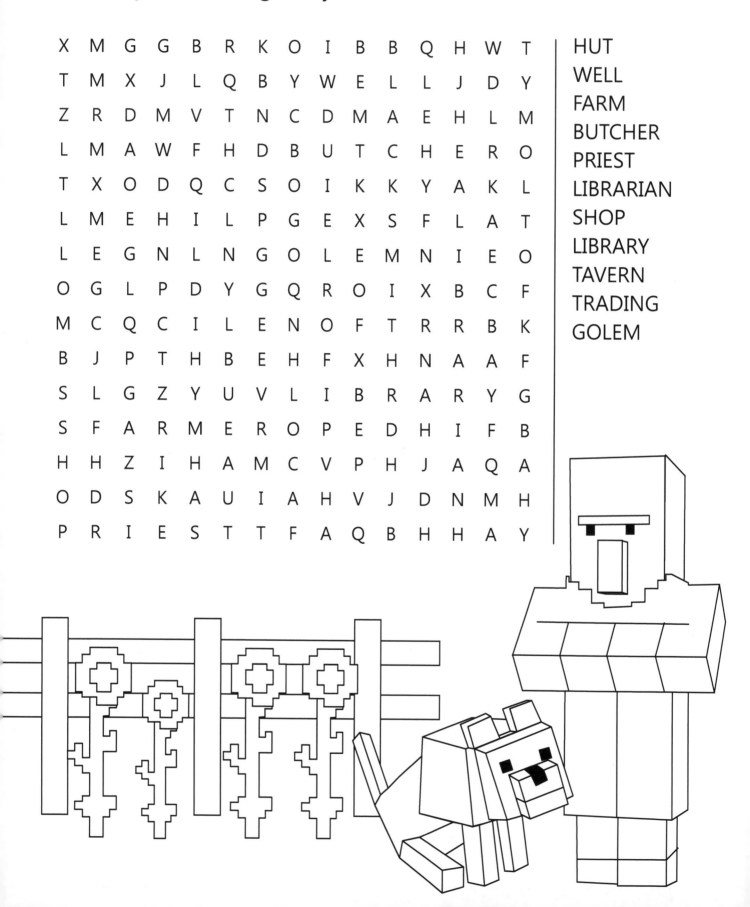

```
X  M  G  G  B  R  K  O  I  B  B  Q  H  W  T
T  M  X  J  L  Q  B  Y  W  E  L  L  J  D  Y
Z  R  D  M  V  T  N  C  D  M  A  E  H  L  M
L  M  A  W  F  H  D  B  U  T  C  H  E  R  O
T  X  O  D  Q  C  S  O  I  K  K  Y  A  K  L
L  M  E  H  I  L  P  G  E  X  S  F  L  A  T
L  E  G  N  L  N  G  O  L  E  M  N  I  E  O
O  G  L  P  D  Y  G  Q  R  O  I  X  B  C  F
M  C  Q  C  I  L  E  N  O  F  T  R  R  B  K
B  J  P  T  H  B  E  H  F  X  H  N  A  A  F
S  L  G  Z  Y  U  V  L  I  B  R  A  R  Y  G
S  F  A  R  M  E  R  O  P  E  D  H  I  F  B
H  H  Z  I  H  A  M  C  V  P  H  J  A  Q  A
O  D  S  K  A  U  I  A  H  V  J  D  N  M  H
P  R  I  E  S  T  T  F  A  Q  B  H  H  A  Y
```

HUT
WELL
FARM
BUTCHER
PRIEST
LIBRARIAN
SHOP
LIBRARY
TAVERN
TRADING
GOLEM

DYES GALORE

Steve wants to color his newly crafted leather armor! Help him find variety of dyes and colors to choose from.

Across:
3. Can get it from bones
4. Sourced from a dandelion or sunflower
5. Sourced from blue orchid
6. A dye obtained through mining
11. Made from poppy or a red tulip
12. Can be crafted from white tulips
13. Made by cooking cactus in a furnace
14. Crafted from allium or lilac
15. Mix cactus green and bone meal

Down :
1. Grows on jungle wood blocks
2. Crafted from rose red and bone meal
7. Dropped by squid
8. Combination of ink sac and bone meal
9. Mix rose red and dandelion yellow
10. Mix rose red and lapis lazuli
13. Combine cactus green and lapis lazuli

NETHER MONSTERS MASH

Identify which characteristic belongs with each Nether mob?

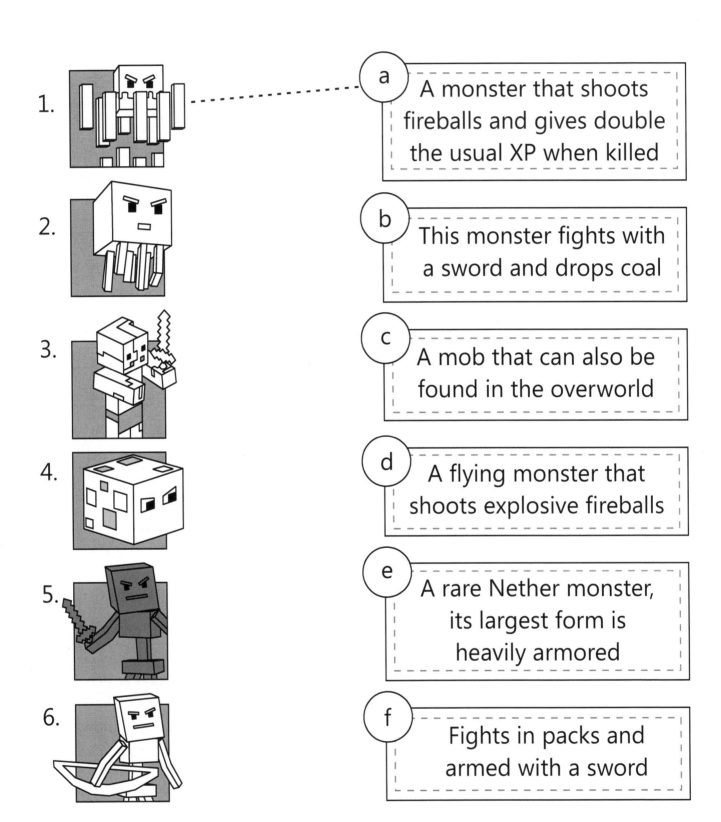

1.

a   A monster that shoots fireballs and gives double the usual XP when killed

2.

b   This monster fights with a sword and drops coal

3.

c   A mob that can also be found in the overworld

4.

d   A flying monster that shoots explosive fireballs

5.

e   A rare Nether monster, its largest form is heavily armored

6.

f   Fights in packs and armed with a sword

59 **GRIEFER THIEF**

Griefer stole five useful items from a bonus chest. Use the code key grid to find out what has been stolen.

1. C1, A4, C2, D3, A1, A5, A5, C1

    -

2. B1, D2, D2, B4, C3

    -

3. A2, A1, C3, B1, D4

    -

4. D1, B1, A1, A1, A5, B2

    -

5. D2, A5, B2, B1, B2, A5

    -

	1	2	3	4	5
A	r	b	i	u	o
B	a	t	m	l	n
C	m	s	e	z	k
D	c	p	h	d	f

JUNGLE MYSTERY

Steve has found a temple hidden deep in the jungle! Help him solve the temple's maze to discover the loot.

ARMOR TYPES

A helmet takes 5 units of armor material to make, a chestplate takes 8, leggings take 7 and boots take 4.

1) How many iron ingots do you need to make 1 full set of iron armor (helmet, chestplate, leggings, boots)?

Answer: ------------------

2) If you have 30 pieces of leather and you want to make sets of armor that only have 1 chestplate and 1 leggings, how many of these sets can you make?

Answer: ------------------

3) If you have 20 gold ingots and you want to make sure that everyone in your team of 5 players has at least one piece of golden armor, what type of armor will you make?

Answer: ------------------

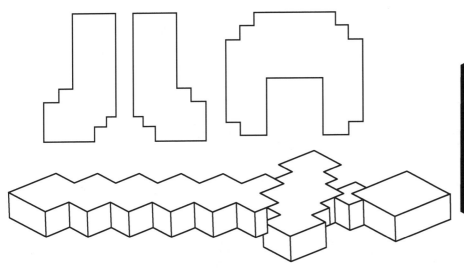

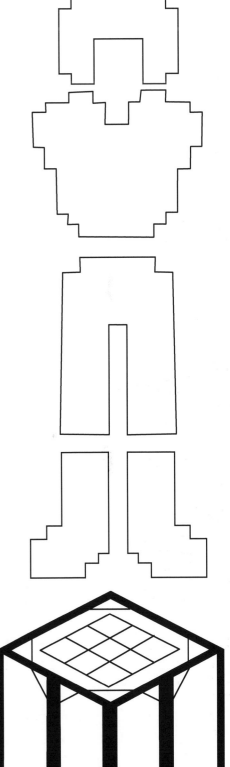

STAMPY CAT PUZZLE

Across:

3. Woolen orange and white tent
4. The name of the dog with red collar
7. A place where Stampy honors his fans
8. Amy Lee's skin
11. Stampy's word for hostile mob
13. Animal that lives on Stampy's balcony
14. Place where Stampy keeps his dogs

Down :

1. Area full of games and rides
2. The name of Stampy's first dog
5. Game that involves a wool rainbow
6. World created by one of Stampy's friends, Crimson Azoth
8. Stampy's only cat friend
9. Provides shelter around the lighthouse area at night
10. Stampy's favorite food
12. Game that is set inside a colorful castle

63 OVERWORLD MONSTERS MASH

Identify which characteristic belongs with each Overworld monster ?

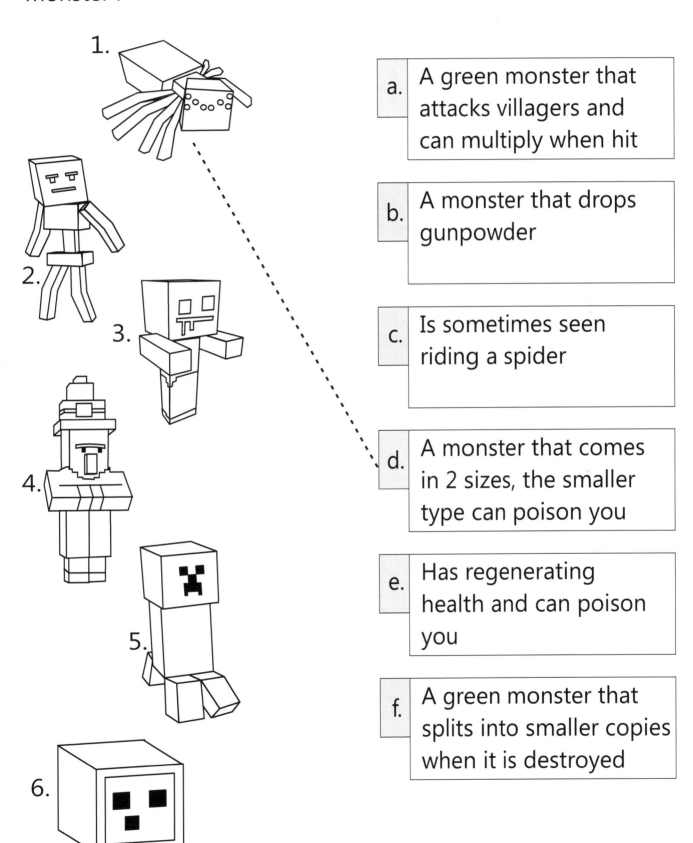

1.

2.

3.

4.

5.

6.

a. A green monster that attacks villagers and can multiply when hit

b. A monster that drops gunpowder

c. Is sometimes seen riding a spider

d. A monster that comes in 2 sizes, the smaller type can poison you

e. Has regenerating health and can poison you

f. A green monster that splits into smaller copies when it is destroyed

USEFUL ITEMS

Finish fitting the letter patterns shown below into the grid to reveal the name of a useful item in each row.

S					
B	U				
H	E	L			

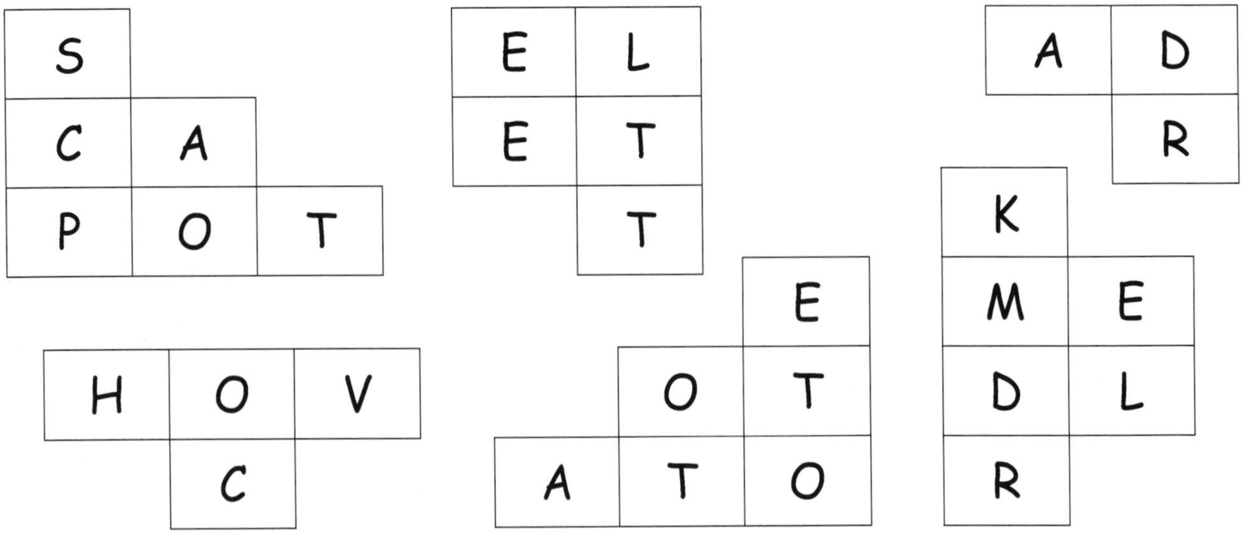

Pieces:

- S / C A / P O T
- H O V / C
- E L / E T / T
- E / O T / A T O
- A D / R
- K / M E / D L / R

MINECRAFT ZOO

Sarah is breeding animals for her Zoo, but they have all escaped! Help her find them before the sunset.

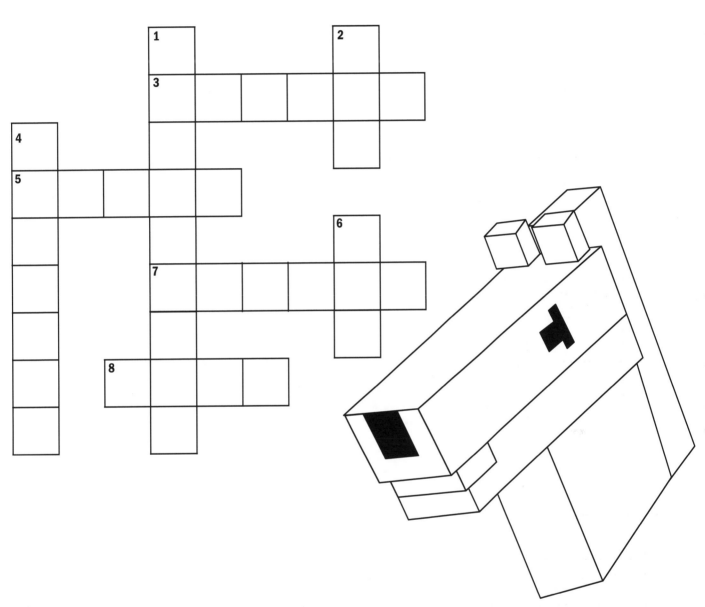

Across :
3. Loves raw fish
5. Can jump very high
7. Hops around aimlessly
8. Tamed by feeding it bones

Down :
1. Red and white spotted animal
2. An animal that you can harvest leather from
4. Egg-laying animal with feathers
6. Can be controlled using a carrot

BIOME BONANZA

Simon took notes on the biomes he encountered on his explorations! Unfortunately his notebook got destroyed in lava, so he has to recreate it from memory. Can you help him remember which biome is which?

1. Ice Plain Spikes ---------
2. Dark Oak Forest ---------
3. Deep Ocean ---------
4. Plains ---------
5. Desert ---------
6. Jungle ---------

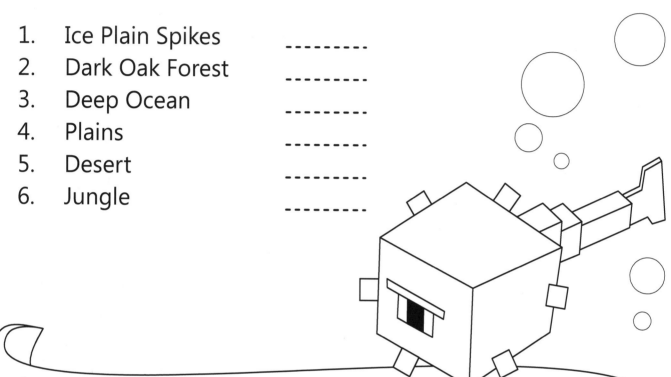

Answers:

a. a rare biome that has massive pillars of hardened ice
b. a biome where horses and sunflowers spawn
c. a biome that contains a lot of gravel and might contain a monument full of guardians
d. the only biome where wild ocelots and melons are found
e. the only biome besides the mushroom island where giant mushrooms are found
f. a biome where water is usually only found in wells

HEALTH REGENERATION

Steve is at 1 health point and he cannot regenerate because he is hungry! He doesn't have normal food, so he has to either eat a golden apple or brew up a potion.

1) A golden apple provides 5 seconds of Regeneration II. If the effect gives Steve one health point every 1.25 seconds, how many golden apples does he need to eat if he wants to fully restore his health bar?

Answer: _____

2) Healing I potion heals 4 health points. Each glistering melon can make 3 Healing I potions. How many glistering melons does Steve need if he plans on consuming only Healing I potions to heal himself to full health?

Answer: _____

3) How many Healing I potions he needs to use to fully restore his health?

Answer: _____

ESSENTIAL TOOLS

Kelly is preparing for her first Minecraft adventure. Help her craft essential tools.

Across :

3. Displays time
5. Used to dig dirt faster
7. Mainly used for obtaining fish
9. Breaks wooden items faster
10. Required to mine all ores

Down :

1. Used to light Nether Portal
2. Used to get wool from sheep
4. Converts dirt and grass blocks into farmland blocks
6. Points to your spawn point
8. Crafted with slimeball and string

OCELOT

Copy the picture of an ocelot by looking closely what is in each square.

NETHER MOBS

Steve is preparing to assault the Nether. What monsters will he face there?

Across:

3. Jellyfish-like creature that lazily hovers around
5. Non fire proof Nether mob
6. Spawns in groups and wanders aimlessly
7. One mob riding on top of another mob

Down:

1. Moves by hopping
2. Drops coal when killed
4. Guards Nether Fortress and shoots fireballs

OCEAN ADVENTURE

Find some of the things you can see during an ocean adventure.

S	W	E	T	S	P	O	N	G	E	R	W	G	R	F
Y	A	T	K	P	B	H	Q	M	K	R	I	U	Q	I
N	O	N	J	B	K	T	T	V	Z	R	B	A	Y	S
C	Q	C	D	S	E	A	L	A	N	T	E	R	N	I
M	Z	K	E	E	O	H	Z	Y	F	N	J	D	W	P
E	X	M	O	A	T	S	Q	U	I	D	H	I	J	I
W	C	T	O	W	N	W	D	R	H	D	Q	A	C	G
W	L	R	T	G	Z	M	A	Z	M	L	W	N	W	Y
C	A	T	L	O	R	M	O	J	I	T	T	H	E	R
U	Y	S	B	G	S	A	F	N	C	L	I	N	V	T
Y	E	K	X	I	H	K	V	L	U	Z	R	I	Q	N
S	F	C	R	W	U	E	U	E	T	M	F	U	U	W
M	M	P	X	I	X	Z	P	D	L	O	E	I	F	Z
O	P	I	R	N	W	H	R	G	R	S	G	N	F	P
R	Z	P	Y	P	R	M	S	W	A	L	Z	G	T	B

CLAY
GRAVEL
GUARDIAN
OCEAN MONUMENT
PRISMARINE
SAND
SEA LANTERN
SQUID
WET SPONGE

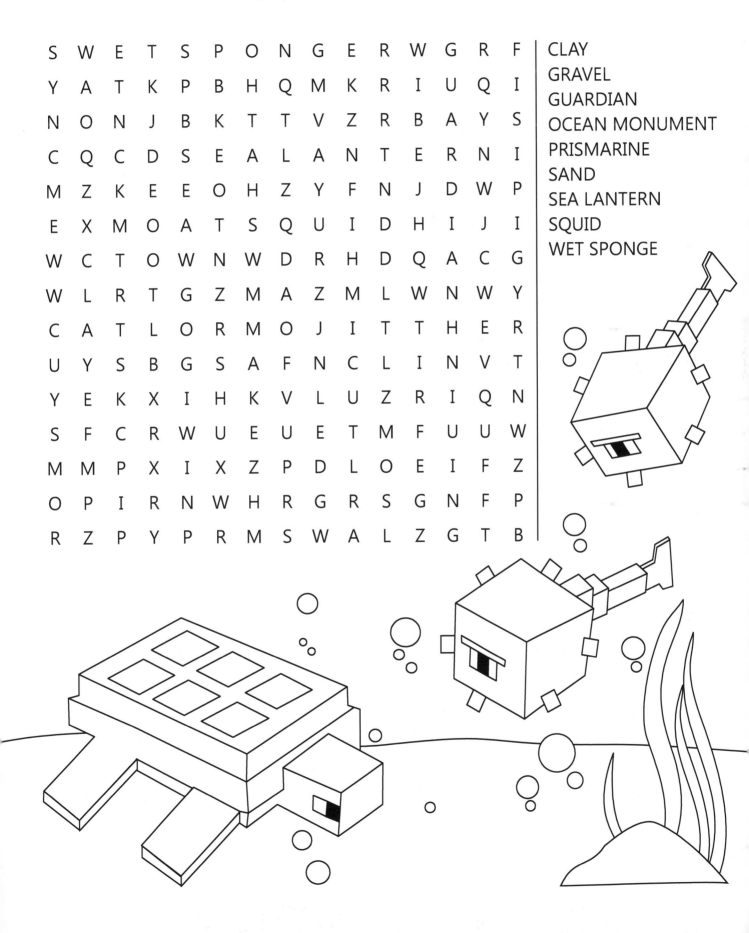

CAVE SPIDER ATTACK

Steve stumbled upon a spider spawner in a cave and wants to use potions of Harming and Healing to fight cave spiders. Harming Potion inflicts 3 hearts of damage and Healing Potion restores 2 hearts. Cave spiders have 6 hearts of health.

1) How many Harming potions Steve needs to throw to destroy a cave spider with full health bar?

Answer: _____

2) Steve is at 2 hearts of health because he was poisoned by a cave spider, how many Healing Potions does he need to consume to fully restore his health bar?

Answer: _____

3) If cave spiders spawn one by one, how many of them can Steve destroy with 24 potions of Harming?

Answer: _____

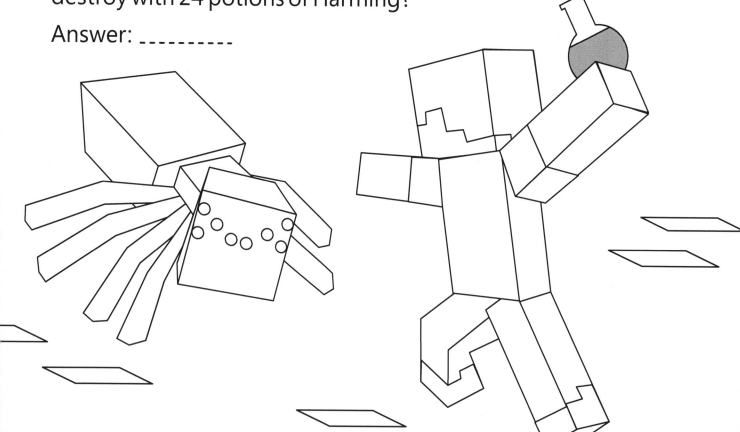

REDSTONE POWER

The words could be written horizontally, vertically or even diagonally!

```
W  C  D  T  Y  M  R  X  T  L  T  F  Q  B  W
H  P  O  Y  R  E  R  L  I  N  G  B  W  F  N
D  T  C  M  V  Z  B  U  T  T  O  N  I  O  O
L  J  Z  E  P  Z  Y  Q  W  U  L  V  T  S  K
P  C  L  T  B  A  D  N  V  Z  Y  S  V  G  C
X  K  D  R  O  P  S  U  E  G  I  K  G  I  R
D  H  D  R  U  H  M  S  Q  P  X  K  M  O  R
D  I  F  B  O  C  I  E  T  B  D  K  O  N  M
T  E  S  K  X  P  G  J  O  A  S  D  C  W  U
L  V  N  P  Q  J  P  A  G  C  P  E  W  W  R
M  A  M  R  E  E  V  E  E  A  L  Z  W  E  N
G  I  S  P  G  N  O  U  R  V  O  O  P  G  F
L  X  W  W  D  A  S  T  Y  H  F  P  C  Q  P
O  O  R  V  K  G  C  E  B  C  O  A  J  K  C
U  O  Y  D  R  M  D  T  R  H  J  O  N  T  N
```

BUTTON
CLOCK
COMPASS
DISPENSER
DROPPER
HOPPER
LEVER
PISTON
TNT
TRAPDOOR

POTION EXPERIMENTS

1) It is 8 am. Steve drinks an 8-minute Strength potion. One minute after the strength runs out, he drinks a 6-minute Night Vision potion. Five minutes later Steve drinks an 8-minute Speed potion. After it runs out, he drinks a 3-minute Jumping potion. When the jumping effect wears off, what time will it be?

Answer: _____

2) How many 3-minute Invisibility potions will Steve have to make if he wants to stay invisible for 24 minutes?

Answer: _____

3) Will he need to make one more to stay invisible for 25 minutes?

Answer: _____

TRANSPORTATION

Sky is reviewing all means of travelling in Minecraft. Find the hidden words in the grid below to help him with that.

```
E A T A G J T N A H N M M R F
P J A M T E L E P O R T E E E
Y Z B M I B U J B Z R A I Z T
M X O S V N D I F P X A A F K
H U A B M C E O C A B W I B W
O C T O B E P C N U A A I L O
V I I Y U M C S A K V L N T S
A X L G P P S W A R E K M K H
B P Y L F O P I H V T Y K K O
U S E N D E R P E A R L R E R
A G U Z J S I T G J G V L A S
N P C J I S N S A A T D E P E
V I U Y Z W T I K L D Y S Z N
Q G Y S C I J E D A I I M B M
F V F W H M X C S B Q U K O E
```

MINECART
RAILS
BOAT
HORSE
DONKEY
PIG
SADDLE
SWIM
SPRINT
WALK
TELEPORT
ENDER PEARL
PORTAL

Hssssssssss!

ANSWERS

1. SPOT THE DIFFERENCE

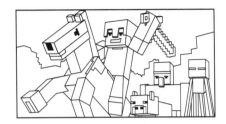

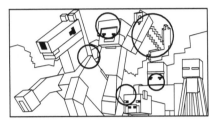

2. THE PICKAXE SHOP

1.e 2.a 3.d 4.c 5.b

3. WHO?

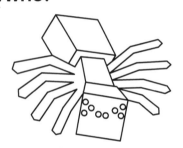

4. NETHER PARKOUR

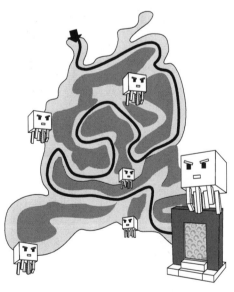

5. HIDDEN PICTURE

6. OCEAN MONUMENT

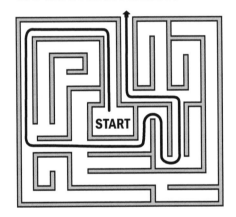

START

7. ENDERMAN PRANK

8. RARE BIOMES

1.d   2.f   3.c
4.e   5.b   6.a

9. MINECRAFT BAKE OFF

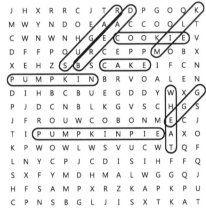

10. SPECIAL MOBS

1.a   2.e   3.d
4.b   5.f   6.c

11. MAGIC PICKAXE

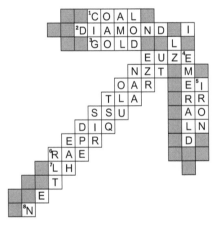

12. SKELETON ATTACK

1) 48 arrows
2) 5 skeletons
3) 28 arrows

13. NETHER SURVIVAL

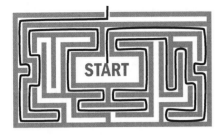

14. CHALET HIDEOUT

Crossword answers:
1. SPRUCE
2. OAK
3. DARK OAK
4. ACACIA
5. JUNGLE
6. BIRCH
7. DYING

15. MARKET DAY

1 emerald left

16. BLURRY VISION

17. NETHER WART MAZE

18. ENDER DRAGON DIGITS

6,   9,   12,   15,   18,
21,   24,   27,   30,   33,
36,   39

19. TRIANGLE ART

20. MUDDLED BIOMES

1. Taiga
2. Forest
3. Desert
4. Mesa
5. Jungle
6. Swampland
7. Savanna
8. Frozen Ocean
9. Extreme Hills
10. Mushroom Island

21. SKELETON DUEL

22. HEDGE MAZE

23. UNDER THE OCEAN

25. FARMING COMPETITION

Across:
5. Pumpkin
7. Poisonous Potato
8. Wheat
9. Carrot
10. Cocoa

Down:
1. Beetroot
2. Melon
3. Sugarcane
4. Mushroom
6. Potato

26. SPIDER ATTACK

27. BREWING INGREDIENTS

1. Ghast Tear
2. Glistering Melon
3. Spider Eye
4. Magma Cream
5. Golden Carrot
6. Blaze Powder
7. Pufferfish
8. Sugar
9. Fermented Spider Eye

29. TRADING

Librarian – Paper
Cleric – Rotten Flesh
Farmer – Wheat
Tool Smith – Diamond
Fisherman – String
Shepherd – Wool

30. VILLAGER BLACKSMITH

Sword

31. WITHER FIGHT

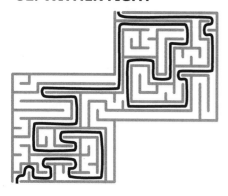

32. RAW FOOD CROSSWORD

Across:
4. Apple
7. Rotten flesh
8. Melon slice
9. Beef
10. Clownfish
11. Pufferfish
12. Carrot
13. Mutton

Down:
1. Spider eye
2. Rabbit
3. Salmon
5. Poisonous
   Potato
6. Chicken

33. STAMPY'S LOVELY
WORLD

Funland

34. CONQUER THE
STRONGHOLD

35. MINECRAFT ARMORY

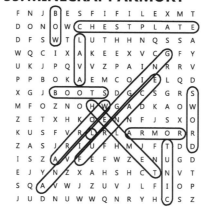

37. FOREST MAZE

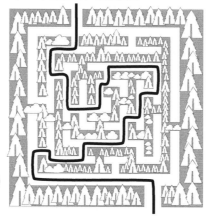

38. POTION BREWING

1. i	2. g	3. d
4. f	5. b	6. c
7. e	8. h	9. a

39. OCELOT FRIEND

40. FURNACE FUEL

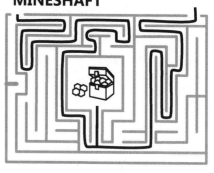

41. ABANDONED
MINESHAFT

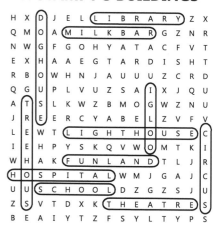

42. BAKING MARATHON

1) 2 cakes
2) 5 buckets of milk
3) 2 slices each; 10 slices
   left over

43. STAMPY'S BUILDINGS

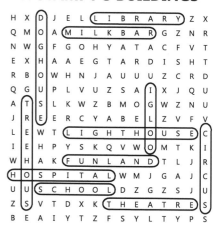

44. SHREDDED NOTE

Gone mining obsidian, will travel to Nether. Need to go to the Nether Fortress to get magma cream for fire resistance potion to fight griefers with lava buckets.

45. TREASURE CHEST

12 coal lumps
3 gold ingots
8 diamonds
16 lapis lazuli
15 iron ingots
3 redstones

46. WHO?

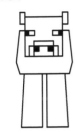

47. FLOWER GARDEN

48. SURVIVAL IN THE NETHER

1) 8 potions
2) 14 potions
3) 5 Regeneration and 2 Strength potions

49. NETHER FORTRESS LOOT

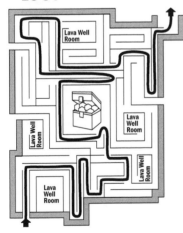

50. VILLAGE PROFESSIONS

1. Cake
2. Saddle
3. Chainmail
4. Bow
5. Eye of Ender
6. Clock

51. MINECRAFT YOUTUBERS

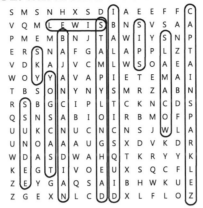

52. CAVE CHALLENGE

53. OVERWORLD HOSTILE MOBS

Across:
1. Killer Rabbit
4. Witch
7. Zombie Villager
8. Slime
9. Skeleton
10. Creeper

Down:
2. Endermite
3. Silverfish
5. Spider Jockey
6. Chicken Jockey
7. Zombie

54. ARMOR STRENGTH

1) 10 hits 2) 5 hits 3) 2 times better

55. DESERT TEMPLE MAZE

56. VILLAGE LIFE

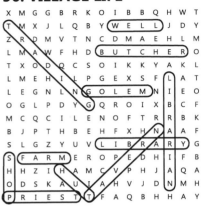

57. DYES GALORE

Across:
3. Bonemeal
4. Dandelion yellow
5. Light blue
6. Lapis Lazuli
11. Rose red
12. Light gray
13. Cactus green
14. Magenta
15. Lime

Down:
1. Cocoa beans
2. Pink
7. Inksac
8. Gray
9. Orange
10. Purple
13. Cyan

58. NETHER MONSTER MASH

1. a   2. d   3. f
4. e   5. b   6. c

59. GRIEFER THEFT

1. mushroom
2. apple
3. bread
4. carrot
5. potato

60. JUNGLE MYSTERY

61. ARMOR TYPES

1) 24 iron ingots
2) 2 sets
3) Boots

62. STAMPY CAT PUZZLE

Across:
3. Circus
4. Barnaby
7. Love garden
8. Mermaid
11. Googly
13. Ester
14. Doghouse

Down:
1. Funland
2. Gregory
5. Raindrops
6. Crimcity
8. Mittens
9. Igloo
10. Cake
12. Flop

63. OVERWORLD MONSTER MASH

1.d, 2. c, 3. a, 4. e, 5. b, 6. f

64. USEFUL ITEMS

S	H	O	V	E	L
B	U	C	K	E	T
H	E	L	M	E	T
S	A	D	D	L	E
C	A	R	R	O	T
P	O	T	A	T	O

65. MINECRAFT ZOO

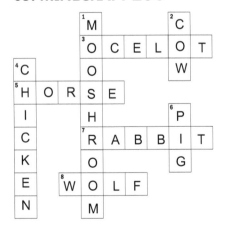

66. BIOME BONANZA

1.a   2. e   3. c
4. b   5. f   6. d

67. HEALTH REGENERATION

1) 5 golden apples
2) 2 glistering melons
3) 5 Healing I potions

68. ESSENTIAL TOOLS

70. NETHER MOBS

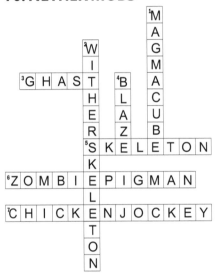

71. OCEAN ADVENTURE

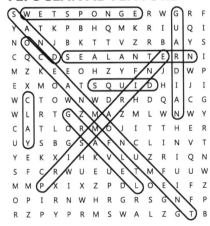

72. CAVE SPIDER ATTACK

1) 2 Harming potions
2) 4 Healing potions
3) 12 cave spiders

73. REDSTONE POWER

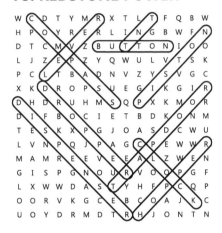

74. POTION EXPERIMENTS

1) 8:25 am
2) 8 Invisibility Potions
3) Yes

75. TRANSPORATION

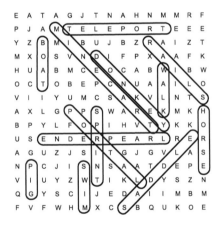

Printed in Great Britain
by Amazon.co.uk, Ltd.,
Marston Gate.